G000124201

CONTENTS

INTRODUCTION

Congratulations on purchasing *How to Train a Puppy* and thank you for doing so.

So, you have decided that you want to raise a puppy. Congratulations! This is a major change in your life that should not be taken lightly. If you are ready to add a puppy to your family, you are committing to taking care of another living creature for the duration of its natural life. You are committing to meeting not only the puppy's physical needs for food, water, and shelter but also socializing your puppy, ensuring that your puppy remains stimulated regularly, and overall making sure the puppy is kept happy.

This can be quite demanding in many ways—puppies, especially when they are young, can require around the clock care and potty breaks, much like how you would have to wake up constantly to take care of a baby. Puppies will not be able to talk to you to tell you what is wrong, and they will always require some degree of care throughout the day just due to the fact that they are not self-sufficient. They cannot let themselves outside unless you happen to have a doggy door. They cannot put food into their own bowls or get themselves water. You will be responsible for another living being's round-the-clock needs.

If that is intimidating to you, you may want to consider some other sort of pet. You may find that you are not actually a dog person, and that is okay. It takes real grace to admit that, and it is better that you take more time to consider just a large decision rather than attempting to force something that will not work out. If it will not work out, that is okay.

Within this book, you will be introduced to everything that you need to know about taking care of a puppy. You will learn what to expect with training a puppy, how the mind of your puppy will work, and why you should make sure that your puppy is a well-trained dog to begin with. You will learn what not to do with your puppy, as well as how to take care of its basic needs. You will be guided through how to teach your puppy everything that he or she needs to know, how to housebreak your puppy, and how to choose which commands your puppy should learn. You will be given several tricks and tips to training your puppy, as well as how to correct some of the most common behavioral problems that you are likely to encounter.

At the end of the day, however, it will be up to you to figure out how to approach this process. You will have to decide what it is that your puppy wants or needs and how to ensure that those needs are met. You will have to determine whether a puppy fits into your lifestyle or if you are setting yourself up for failure in trying to bring them into your life to begin with. Hopefully, by the time you have finished reading this book, you will know whether you have made the right and responsible decision to bring a dog into your life in the first place.

TRAINING A PUPPY: EVERYTHING YOU NEED TO KNOW

PUPPIES, like people, learn in stages. They develop over time, much like people do. They require constant supervision in the early days and behave much like a destructive toddler. If you think you can leave your puppy alone unsupervised while you go to work all day, think again—just as you cannot leave a toddler alone unsupervised for an extended period of time, you cannot leave your puppy home alone either.

*H*owever, unlike a child, a puppy can be trained much quicker. Thanks to the fact that puppies reach maturity far sooner than people do, the periods of time in which your puppy is entirely and utterly reliant on you to keep him or her from destroying things is much lower, so long as you put the work in. You must be willing and able to train your pup in order to ensure that he or she will be able to understand his or her place and role in the house and in your family. To some degree, this will involve understanding dominance and your dog—recognizing how it becomes critically important for you to make sure that all humans rank higher in the hierarchy than the dog does. However, that does not mean that you need to be aggressive—we will be going over the difference between assertiveness and aggressiveness later within this book.

*W*ithin this chapter, we are going to address what training a puppy will generally look like. We will go over how a dog sees the world so you will be able to ensure that your own training is successful in the first place. We will go over the benefits of having a well-trained dog, and go over the importance of choosing a breed that fits the lifestyle that you live. No two breeds of dogs are identical, and the sooner you recognize this, the sooner you will be able to make those important changes that you would like to see.

*T*raining Puppies

Training puppies is not necessarily a difficult thing to do —but it is something that can become quite tedious if you are not particularly engaged in the process. It is absolutely hard work—but it is absolutely critical to your puppy's development. Ultimately, your puppy will rely on you to make him or her the perfect canine citizen. He or she will be dependent upon you to sculpt his or her behavior into that of a well-behaved dog. Ultimately, this world is quite intolerant of dogs that are not well-behaved. They are expected to be trained well firstly due to a safety issue if a dog is not properly trained and socialized, but secondly due to assuming that your dog will have good manners when you do take it out and about.

. . .

*W*hen you are going to be training your puppy, you are looking to do so in very short periods at any given point in time. You are going to be wanting to incorporate training as soon as you get your pup. You may be using simple obedience training, for example, to encourage and facilitate your dog in becoming accustomed to listening to you. You may be teaching simple commands such as sit or stay. Ultimately, you are going to want to do this training several times throughout the day for roughly 5 minutes at a time. They do not have very long attention spans, especially in those early days, and you want to make sure that you are regularly encouraging and facilitating that training through repetition. This will help you to reinforce the training as it is happening.

*W*hen you are training, the key is ensuring that it is something positive. It should be positive and happy, with you doing your best to focus on positive reinforcement as it happens. This will not only help strengthen the bond between you and your puppy, it will also allow for your puppy to learn better sooner.

The Inner Workings of the Dog's Mind

It may come as a shock to you, but a dog does, in fact, think. Dogs, once they are fully grown, usually have the same level of cognition that you would expect to see in a child between the ages of 3 and 5. They are capable of recognizing what you are pointing at. They can tell which bowl of food or water has more than another. They can tell what is going on with body language. They will naturally pick up on how to communicate with you in ways that you can recognize and understand yourself.

*H*owever, even with that sort of cognition capability, you will find that your dog cannot be reasoned with in the way that you would reason with a 3-year-old child. You cannot tell your dog not to climb onto the furniture because you do not like the fur that is all over it. What you can do, however, is work on how to teach your dog to follow through with what you want. You will want to find that dogs and puppies are quite capable of learning about the world around them, but that learning will happen somewhat differently.

*Y*ou will want to be focusing on either giving your dog positive attention or not at all to get the point across with your dog's behavior. This means that telling your dog no and scolding it is not likely to be effective, but what you can do is ignore your dog entirely when they are doing something that they should not be doing. This is because your dog wants to please you. Dogs are literally bred to please us—they developed and evolved alongside humans to become reliant on us and therefore, they look to us on a regular basis. You will be able to keep this in mind when you are training your dog. Remember that you are asserting yourself as the calm, in-charge leader. Your dog will need gentle but firm redirection and training from you. Your dog will feel more secure when you are able to be firm and clear with boundaries and with expectations, especially when they are consistent. All of this must be remembered if you want to hope to train your pup into a well-behaved canine citizen.

The Benefits of Having a Well-Trained Dog

When you train your puppy, you are creating all sorts of benefits, both for yourself and for your dog. You are ensuring that you are meeting your dog's need to be able to fit in—you are ensuring that your dog is able to become a well-behaved member of your family by ensuring that your dog knows how to meet your expectations. When you train your dog to be obedient, you ensure that your dog is going to look to you—you will be in complete control of your dog. This is powerful because it allows you to establish yourself as the leader that your dog will be looking up to. When you do this, you ensure that your dog is going to be looking to you regularly. You ensure that your dog is entirely interested in your own interpretations of the world around it and that your dog wants to please you. This is important for all sorts of reasons, such as:

- **Safety:** A dog that you cannot control can do a lot of damage. People can, and regularly do, die from dog attacks, and many of these deaths can actually be prevented if the dogs are taken care of and trained properly. Of course, your dog is a living, breathing creature that is capable of acting unpredictably, but most of the time, when you have a dog that you have trained well, they will listen to you, even if they do not necessarily want to at that point in time. You will be able to recall your dog to get them back to your side. You will be able to ensure that they do not snarl over their food bowl when your toddler inevitably tries to reach into it while your dog is eating. You will make sure that your dog will not jump up on people and hurt them. Especially if you have a dog that is larger, you are going to want to ensure that it is well trained for everyone's safety —your dog's included.
- **Control:** A dog that you cannot control is a dog that is a risk to other people. Your dog may run away if you cannot control him. Your dog may try to attack a cat if you cannot

recall him. Your dog may harass other people or bark incessantly if you cannot command him to be quiet. Some of these may be simple annoyances, but others can pose real safety risks as well. You need to be able to control your dog to ensure that your dog does not impact other people.

- **Bonding:** When you are working on training your puppy, you are facilitating a strong bond built on trust. You are teaching your dog that you are someone that can be looked up to and trusted, and that will make your dog calmer and more confident. Dogs thrive in settings where there are strict rules and expectations. When you can ensure that your dog is likely to follow those rules and expectations, you can make sure that your dog bonds to you better.

- **Easier time taking your dog out:** When you have a dog, you may decide that you want to take him or her out places. Whether it is to the park, the dog park, or on a trip and into a hotel for the weekend, you need a dog that is well behaved. When you ensure that your dog is, in fact, well trained, you will be able to do this with ease because your dog will have better manners.

- **Better socialization skills:** When you train your dog the right way, you ensure that he or she learns all of those important social skills in life that will allow your dog to go out and spend time with other dogs. When a dog is not well trained, it can end up pestering other dogs or acting in ways that other dogs deem inappropriate, making it difficult, or even impossible in some situations, to create those interactive settings between your dog and others.

Choosing a Breed That Is Right for You

As one final point to consider within this chapter, you must learn how to identify what kind of dog is right for you to begin with. This will be incredibly important for you—you need to ensure that the dog that you choose is one that will fit in with your lifestyle just due to the fact that there are so many different breeds of dogs out there. In fact, there are right around 200 dog breeds out there that are currently recognized by the AKC, and then you have to consider all of the mixed breeds and mutts that exist as well. This means that you have many different options out there for you to decide between.

When you are trying to choose a dog for your own family, there are many different considerations that you will need to make to ensure that ultimately, the dog that you have chosen is one that will fit neatly into your own current lifestyle. Let's go over a few of the different considerations that you need to make.

Your Experience With Dogs

Some dogs are naturally more obedient than others. Some dogs, such as Huskies and Shiba Inus are dogs that will require far more effort and experience than a dog that naturally wants to please you. If you are reading this book, there is a very good chance that you are a beginner to owning a puppy on your own, and because of that, you should aim for a breed that is usually going to be deemed easygoing or easy to train.

· · ·

Your Space Available to You

Just because you are in a city apartment without a yard does not mean that you cannot get a dog. In fact, many different breeds of dogs can actually do great inside without a yard, so long as you are willing and able to take them out to run around on a regular basis. Consider breeds that are going to be better suited to apartment life when you are doing your research if you live in one. If you have a yard, consider how big and how secure it is as well.

Your Current Family Dynamic

Another point to consider when trying to choose your dog will be whether or not you have children and whether those children are younger and therefore more likely to annoy your dog at some point or another. Some dogs do great with children—for example, golden retrievers are often considered the quintessential family dog due to their patience with children. Other dogs, however, such as Chihuahuas, may get nippy with children that they perceive as a threat.

How Much Noise You Can Tolerate

Dogs can vary greatly in terms of how vocal they will become and you will have to decide just how much noise you are willing and able to accept from them. You must decide if constant barking and whining is going to be a problem for you or if you want a dog that is largely quiet and will only bark when needed. This is going to be up to personal preference. While you may be able to influence just how loud or quiet your dog may be, you will find that some breeds are generally much yappier than others.

How Much Maintenance Is Required

You may need to also consider if you want a dog that will require meticulous grooming or one that is going to be more clean than not. Some dogs will shed more than others. Some dogs will require regular bathing and haircuts. Some dogs will drool all over the place, and other dogs will be relatively low maintenance. You must know exactly how much you are willing to put up with so you can make an informed decision.

How Big of a Dog You Want

You will also need to be well aware of how large of a dog that you want, or if you live in a rental unit, how large of a dog you can have. Many rental units have rules in place that limit the size of dogs within their apartments and you will need to consider this yourself. You will also need to consider that larger dogs will usually eat more and may also require more space and exercise than smaller dogs, though that is not always the case. Larger dogs may also be more difficult to control when unruly than smaller ones—for example, you may be able to lift up a Chihuahua that is harassing someone, but if your lab goes running after someone and you are a relatively small person, you may find that you are yanked along without any real recourse.

How Active You Are or Are Willing to Be

Finally, as one last point to consider, you may want to

look at dogs that have a similar exercise and activity level to what you already have going on in your life. If you are a couch potato, you are not going to want to adopt a big working dog under the assumption that getting said big working dog will help you feel motivated to get off the couch and go work out. You do not know if that is the case—you may get lazy about it, or you may decide that it is not worth the effort and then you have a dog that you are not taking care of properly. Some dogs will be perfectly happy being couch potatoes along with you, so long as you give them a quick 10- minute walk, but others will insist on much more exercise, with some of the working breeds needing at least an hour or two of vigorous exercise throughout the day.

WHAT NOT TO DO

As we begin to move along, it becomes important to begin looking at some of the most common puppy training mistakes that get made on a regular basis. Consider this your guide on exactly what NOT to do when you get your puppy and first bring him or her home. They will only make life more difficult for you and can actually seriously hinder your attempts to train your puppy at all. Let's take a look at some of the most common mistakes now.

You Use the Command, "No, [Puppy's Name]"

This is a major mistake for one particular reason: When you are constantly pairing, "no," with your puppy's name, you are teaching your dog that they should associate their name with the word, "No." This is a problem—you have suddenly taught your pup that his name is something to be afraid of or something to be avoided or stopped. Instead of your dog being happy to see you or hear you call his name, your dog will instead be hesitant—he will hear his name and freeze up, assuming that he has done something wrong to begin with, and that will seriously hurt you and your pup's relationship later down the line.

*Y*ou Use the Command, "No," At All

Similarly, you may find that you eliminate this command altogether. No is an incredibly nonspecific command. While we understand the nuances behind the word and we understand that it means that you are telling the dog not to do that one activity that they are just doing that moment, your dog does not get the message. Remember, your dog does not speak English—to your dog, telling him no could sometimes mean to get down, but other times mean to be quiet. Sometimes, the command is used to get the dog to stop barking, but other times the command is used to tell him to stop running. It is incredibly confusing for a dog that does not understand what it is that you are asking him or her to do in the first place and because of that, you should try to eliminate this command from your vocabulary.

*I*nstead, try teaching your dog other commands that can be used. If you are trying to tell your dog that they cannot jump on the couch with you, you could try telling your dog, "Down," instead. That is a very specific command that always has the same exact result: Your dog puts all feet on the floor. When you use a very specific command with your pup instead of trying to teach them nonspecific words, you will find that they better understand what your expectation is and because of that, they are better able to meet those expectations in the first place.

. . .

You Don't Start Training Immediately

Dog training should start almost immediately upon arriving home. It used to be believed that you should not start it until somewhere between 6 months and a year, but nowadays, it is known that waiting that year is a good way to solidify all sorts of bad behaviors that you would otherwise like to avoid. Instead of allowing your puppy to run rampant until he or she is older, recognize that you can start training on day 1. You can teach your pup to recognize and respect boundaries early on, and starting immediately gives your pup a head start over his or her peers. When you are already actively attempting to train your pup on how to behave, you know that your pup is going to be that much more likely to follow behaviors later on because you have already set that foundation for yourself.

You Don't Want to Be Inconsistent With Commands

Some people may find it hard to resist repeating their commands over and over again. They may be trying to get their dog to stay, for example, by saying, "Stay. Stay. Stay. Stay. Stay." However, there is a problem with this—when you are repeating yourself over and over again, you are teaching your dog that they need to follow your commands, but only after you have repeated that command several times over, and that is a problem. When you do this with your dog, you will teach him or her that the command is not simply, "Stay." But rather, repeating the world five times over, and they will not actively stay until you do exactly that —tell them to stay five times in a row.

. . .

*Y*ou Punish Your Puppy When You Discover the Problem

Oftentimes, people do not realize that their puppy has done something undesirable until after the fact. Perhaps you found that your favorite shoe has been chewed up earlier in the day, so you go stomping over to your pup, shove your chewed-up shoe in the pup's face and start to scold him. However, there is a problem with this—dogs think in the moment. They do not really understand what it is that they did earlier, nor do they realize or understand that you are currently scolding behavior that happened earlier. They think that you are scolding what they are doing in that particular moment rather than what they did earlier and you are missing the lesson.

*T*his goes double for potty training—if you find that your pup has had an accident, you cannot walk your pup over to said accident and attempt to scold him or her. You cannot make it clear to your pup that you are angry about the accident in any way—not even by rubbing his or her nose in it, which is something that you should never, ever do under any circumstance.

*Y*ou Use Physical Discipline

Some people think that since they cannot speak and reason with their dogs, the only way that they have to get their point across is with physical discipline in an attempt to get them to submit. However, this is not the case. All that happens when you attempt to dominate your dog through such methods is that you teach your dog not to trust you at all, damaging your relationship with him or her and making it harder for you to really bond.

Calling Your Dog to You for Discipline

Another mistake that all too many people make is calling their dog to them when they plan on doing something unpleasant. Whether you are going to be scolding your dog, calling them for bath time, or to get in the car to go to the vet, when you call your dog to you in order to do something that your dog will not enjoy, you run the risk of making them decide that they will avoid you. They will not want to come to you when they know that sometimes, going to you is not the pleasant thing that it should be. They will see it as something that is quite possibly unpleasant, so they avoid it whenever possible.

Treating Your Dog Like a Person

People will oftentimes personalize their dog. They will treat their dog like they would treat their children—and this is a problem. Firstly, your dog is not your child. Your dog is not a human. Your dog does not think like a human or have the wants of a human. Your dog is certainly deserving of the same respect that you would afford any other living being, but you should not be allowing your dog to do whatever he or she wants. When your dog looks at you like an equal rather than a leader, you are going to set your dog up to rebel when he or she wants. Your dog may feel like you are not the one in control of all of these different situations around him or her and because of that he will begin to take liberties that you would rather not afford. For this particular reason, it is important to remember that your dog is a dog and that is it.

THE CARE AND KEEPING OF YOUR PUPPY

WITH THOSE COMMON mistakes behind you, it is time to begin looking at some of the most important ways in which you will be caring for your puppy. We are going to be going over general guidelines for all of the general care and keeping of your dog. We are going to be addressing how to groom your puppy, how to pick out food for your puppy, how to exercise your puppy, how to play with your puppy, how often to take your puppy out to relieve him or herself, and how to train your puppy. Each of these is incredibly important aspects of puppy ownership and if you cannot recognize how to meet these needs with your own pup, you are going to find that you struggle.

Grooming Your Puppy

Grooming pups is something that should happen depending upon their coats. Some pups only need occasional baths while others may need more. As a general rule, your pup will need a bath or grooming once a month. You may decide to do this yourself, or you may find that you are better off paying for a groomer to take care of it.

*G*enerally speaking, when you take your dog to a groomer, your dog will get the whole treatment in one. They will be able to bathe your pup, as well as brush and dry them. They will be able to clean your dog's ears out to ensure that there is no earwax, and also make sure that any trimming of fur or hair is done. Beyond just that, there will be trimming done for your dog's toenails, and usually, the teeth will also be brushed.

*O*f course, you can choose to do all of this yourself at home, as well. You will just need to make sure that you have all of the tools to do so. You will want to look up a guide on your specific dog's breed to get more information about what will be required and how you can ensure that your pup's hygiene is always taken care of. Generally speaking, however, you will want to ensure that you have a good brush specific to your pup's fur type, which can vary greatly from breed to breed. You will need to have shampoo designed for use on dogs in particular, who may have much more sensitive skin than you do. You will want to ensure that you use guillotine-style clippers for your dog's nails and you will need to be careful not to clip the quick to avoid bleeding. Just in case, however, you will want to have styptic powder on hand in case you do happen to trim too short and hit the quick to cause bleeding. You may find, especially if you have a dog that sheds a lot, that it is easier just to take him or her to the groomer once a month than it is to deal with everything else yourself, and that is okay! No matter what, however, you will want to ensure that your pup is getting cleaned up regularly.

Feeding Your Puppy

Another important aspect of dog ownership is ensuring that your pup is getting the right nutrition at all times. This means that you will need to figure out exactly what it is that your pup needs to be fed and happy. This will largely vary from pup to pup and you are going to be best served looking up what kind of food and diet is going to be best for the breed that you have. Generally speaking, any of the food that you get at the pet store will be at the very least of a good enough quality to be fed to your pup—it will be edible. However, that is about as much as you can really determine. Some dog food is going to be better than others—some dog food is packed up full of grains and scraps that are not particularly nutritious for your pup. They may be full of fillers and some multivitamins that are meant to balance them out. Other dog foods will be made with meat instead of meat byproducts and they will generally be a bit healthier for your pup to be consuming. As a general rule, the more expensive the dog food that you get, the higher the quality generally is. This is not a hard and fast rule, however—what is going to matter more is that the food is going to be made of whole food products instead of byproducts or animal meal. When you can make sure that you are choosing the right sorts of food, you will be able to ensure that the food that your pup is getting is going to be healthier in general for him.

Of course, if you have the time to do so, the best choice for pups will almost always be having their dog food homemade. This will require you to figure out exactly what your particular dog's nutritional requirements will be, however, and you will want to ensure that you can do this by learning what you can online. You will then have to look into how to balance out that nutritional requirements with your own whole foods. This is a bit more time consuming at first, and it may be costlier than other options, but will probably be the healthiest for your dog. Over time, you will get the experience that you will need to simply make a batch of dog food once a week, or even once a month if you decide to freeze and store it, and you will know exactly what your pup is eating.

*A*s well as ensuring that your pup is fed, usually to a schedule, you will want to make sure that you always have water available for him or her to drink. Usually, your pup will take care to drink as needed so you will not have to worry too much about whether he or she is getting enough water. Nevertheless, you will want to keep an eye to make sure that he or she is, in fact, drinking at all. Some pups struggle to drink with deep bowls and you may need to try providing a shallower dish for them to drink from.

*E*xercising Your Puppy

Dogs of all kinds need exercise. They need this to keep them healthy and strong. The amount of exercise may vary greatly from dog to dog, but they will still need to get up and active at least for some period of time each day. Most dogs are not likely to exercise themselves even if you do allow them to go outside—you will need to be actively engaging with your dog and following your dog to ensure that he or she is actually doing what he is doing. Most dogs need somewhere between 30 minutes and 2 hours of exercise within a day, depending on the breed. Working dogs will generally require more, whereas smaller dogs will typically not require much at all.

· · ·

*E*xercise can be facilitated in many different ways. You may, for example, exercise your dog with a leisurely walk through the neighborhood a few times a day. Other dogs, however, will have much more vigorous needs and may require you to actively hike or work them. Your pup, if you do not exercise him or her adequately is likely to fall into all sorts of negative or destructive behaviors, which is precisely the reason why you *do* need to be mindful of what you are doing with them and ensuring that they are being worked enough. When they are not worked enough, they will oftentimes find other ways to burn that energy that you would rather not deal with.

*P*laying with Your Puppy

Playing with your pup is another regular expectation that you need to meet. Your pup or dog will always want to spend time with you, and that time will be spent in all sorts of different ways. Your pup may want to play tug-o-war with you or play fetch with you. No matter how you chose to play with your dog, however, you are facilitating a better bond with them. You will be able to make your dog feel more bonded and attached to you when you are regularly sharing these sorts of positive interactions with each other and those positive interactions are what you are looking to see with them.

*O*f course, this playtime is also a great way for you to facilitate more exercise as well. It can be a way for you to kill two birds with one stone—you can play fetch at the dog part, for example, encouraging your pup to get up, on his feet, and running around. You can get your pup actively running and in doing so, you will find that he or she is going to be happier in general. Your pup will feel like that social need has been met and that is incredibly important.

*O*nce again, if you do not take the time to play with your dog to keep him or her socially and mentally stimulated, you are going to find that you wind up with a destructive dog. Your dog will not be very well behaved if he or she is bored. You ultimately want to wear your dog out. A tired dog is always going to be a good dog.

*T*aking Your Puppy Outside

You may be wondering now how often you need to worry about taking your pup out to use the bathroom. Generally speaking, a pup can hold their bladder for roughly as many hours as the age they are, plus one. This means that a two-month-old puppy should never be expected to hold it longer than three hours, and if you really want to be successful at training them, you are going to want them to go out even more regularly. You will want to aim for every hour or two for young puppies during the day, and then every 3 or so hours at night. Yes, this means that you are going to be waking up throughout the night for the first few months—if you are not prepared for this, you may decide that you will get a puppy that is older, or that you will adopt an adult dog, which is always an option as well.

*G*enerally speaking, you will want to take your pup outside right after eating or drinking, right after waking up, and right after he or she has been playing for a while. These are the most likely times that your pup is going to want to go to relieve him or herself, and you are going to want to take your pup out more often than he or she will need to avoid running into problems with accidents later on.

*Y*ou will also want to look for any signs that your pup needs to go out as well—you will usually see signs such as pacing, whining, or walking in circles. Some pups will also sniff at the ground to find a suitable spot. If you see any of this, assume that it is a potty emergency and get your pup out immediately. If you do happen to mistime things and end up with an accident, ensure that you clean it up promptly with enzyme cleaners that are designed to eliminate the scent of waste. If you do not entirely destroy the odor in that area, your pup will go back to that spot to go, over and over again.

*T*raining Your Puppy

Finally, the last major point of the day-to-day care of your pup is going to be ensuring that you are following through with your training of him or her. This is something that we are going to be looking at in-depth shortly—it involves ensuring that your pup is being taught what is expected on a regular basis. You will want to ensure that your training starts immediately, and once you do start to train your pup, you want to ensure that you remain consistent and reliable. You will want to make sure that you are constantly practicing those behaviors that you are attempting to facilitate and that you are ensuring that your pup is learning the commands that he or she needs. Just like with potty training, you will want to ensure that your training is being constantly reinforced. You may even start to begin a routine in which you work on obedience training for a few short minutes each and every time that your pup comes in from relieving him or herself. When you can do this on the regular, you will find that your pup is much more likely and willing to follow along with what you are suggesting. This is absolutely a need for your pup that must be met just as often as the needs for food and water.

TEACHING YOUR PUPPY

WHEN YOU ARE ready to train your puppy, there are a few key points to remember if you really want to be successful. These points will help you make sure that you are effective in how you interact with your puppy and be as firm and fair of a leader as you can to him or her. Ultimately, people are commonly making many of the mistakes that we have gone over thus far in the book. People will find that they repeatedly make these mistakes over and over again and as a result, they find that they wind up with a puppy that is poorly trained in some way. However, you can learn to mitigate that by remembering the five principles that you will be given in this chapter.

The Importance of Positivity

Positivity is almost always more effective at long-term training than negativity. Imagine, for example, that you want to train your pup to stay off of your couch. Now, your couch is comfortable. Your couch is also where you are sitting, and your pup is going to naturally want to be around you because he or she loves you. Let's say that your puppy decides to jump up on the couch. What do you do next?

*Y*ou can now choose whether you are going to respond negatively to this—you may yell at the pup, throw something at the pup, push the pup off of the couch, or all of the above. For the record, none of this is treatment that your pup should be enduring at all, but consider it for the point of this example. This is all negative training. You are making the stimulus of jumping onto the couch negative in hopes that your pup will learn not to do it at all. There are even products these days designed to do just that. However, your pup isn't learning to stay off of the couch—your pup is learning to stay off of the couch when you are around. He is afraid of your response and so he avoids it as much as he can when he knows you are around.

*W*hen you use positive training, however, you encourage your pup to recognize something—you are teaching your pup that you are happier when your pup is on the floor. You gently put the pup on the floor and pat his head and offer a treat and some praise. This tells your pup that good things happen when all feet are on the floor as opposed to bad things happening when he tries to climb up when you are around.

*P*ositive training then becomes much more motivational. Your pup learns to associate the training that you want with good things—praise, treats, and attention. All of those are great motivators for pups. They are entirely happy to receive it, which is precisely why you should consider doing things in this manner.

The Importance of Consistency

Beyond just remaining positive with your puppy, you must also ensure that you are always consistent. Dogs thrive on consistency. Consistency is predictable, regulates their expectations, and allows them to know exactly what they can and cannot do. When you are training your pup, that means that you must always use the same commands as everyone else that is currently training. Make sure that everyone is using the same words, the same methods, and the same rewards for the commands you are training.

You will also want to ensure that you get your puppy on some sort of a schedule that will aid you in ensuring that your pup learns to do what is needed with ease. You can do this by making it a routine to take your pup out at certain times, followed by a predictable schedule of training, feeding, playing, and napping. When you keep your pup on a consistent schedule, you know that you r pup is comfortable with what is happening around you. You and your pup will be able to act with each other in perfect sync when you learn how to line up those expectations and consistency.

The Line Between Firm and Harsh

Another important thing to consider is the difference between firm and being harsh. You can be quite firm without ever saying or doing anything mean. You can also be quite harsh

26

without saying a mean word. When you are talking to your pup, you want to ensure that you are always firm with him or her. In remaining firm, you can assert that you are in control and that is important. You need to be able to remain in control so your pup knows that he or she can count on you. Your pup will naturally turn to you—his instincts tell him that you are in charge, especially when you do take back that control and power, and when you can work with that with ease, you will show your pup that he can trust you.

*H*owever, when you are too harsh with your pup, you run the risk of scaring him. You need to recognize that the difference between assertion and aggression is exceedingly slim, but it is one that matters greatly. Assertion and ensuring that your pup knows what you are expecting is one thing, but snapping at your pup and yelling at him for getting something wrong is an entirely different matter altogether.

*B*eing firm involves being calm. You must be calm in order to interact with your pup in a way that is not going to upset him. This is because your pup will pick up on your stress. Your pup will know when you are not happy and that stresses your pup out, too. Your pup wants to be able to know that you are happy—he wants to please you. However, he cannot do that if he does not know what he is doing or how he should. Assertion is calm and firm. Aggression is the result of anger mixing in with assertion. Keep this in mind and make sure that you always do your best to respond in a way that is calm.

The Right Tone

When you are training your pup, tone is everything. Firstly, your pup knows what a harsh tone is—it will immediately put your pup on the defensive and no good learning happens when that occurs. You need your pup to be able to understand you and be in a learning mood for you to be able to train him, but being harsh or angry is not going to do that.

*W*hen you are talking to your pup, you want to use higher-pitched tones. Dogs in general naturally tend to gravitate toward those tones. They respond well to whistles, for example, because the whistle cuts through everything else and allows the pup to focus on one thing in particular. This means that you should also speak to your pup in a tone that is higher as well. Not only are higher tones usually perceived as more positive and pleasant, your pup will be able to better make out your words.

*T*hink about how people speak to toddlers—their voices go up an octave or so and they slow down their speech a bit. This is what you want to do when you are talking to your pup. You can forget about all of that baby talk nonsense where you start asking if Spotty-wotty-baby wants to go on walkie. You can use full, regular words when you are talking to your pup without you having to degrade down to full-blown baby gibberish. Use regular words, but try to make them short when you use this tone.

*R*ewards Versus Punishment

Finally, one last thing to remember when you are training your puppy is that you need to remember the difference between punishment and rewarding. When you focus on being rewarding for good behavior, you are much more likely to encourage those good behaviors that you want to see in your pup. You are much more likely to get your pup to go along with you and what you are wanting to do if your pup can see that he or she is likely to get a reward for those good behaviors.

*W*hen you focus on making sure that behaviors that you like are rewarded, you encourage your pup to repeat them again and again. Your pup will see that those behaviors were worthwhile because they led to both of you getting exactly what you wanted out of the situation. You are happy, which is a reward for your pup on its own, but you also offered your pup some sort of reward or treat for doing what he should have done. That encourages your pup further in the future to repeat those behaviors. You should always work on rewarding the positive to encourage those behaviors more in the future rather than making them neutral. You want your pup to feel driven to performing those behaviors because those behaviors are the ones that you want to see.

*P*unishment does not teach the pup what to do—it teaches the pup what *not* to do, which is exceedingly vague. Imagine that you walk into a room and there is a strange item that you have never seen before sitting on a table and you are told to use it. You may not know what it is or what it is for. Now, imagine that you ask them what it is meant for. They then tell you what it is *not* for, without ever specifying what you should do with it. Do you know what you should be doing now?

•   •   •

*T*he chances are, no. You do not know what you should be doing with it. You have no idea what it is that you need to do with it and being told what else not to do did not help you get any closer to figuring out that proper behavior. You see this oftentimes with people using the command, "No." You may know that the command is good for telling someone to stop doing what they are doing, but for a dog, they are confused. They need you to specify what you want them to do, and punishing the behaviors that are wrong does not help them.

HOUSEBREAKING YOUR PUPPY

NEXT, it is time to look into housebreaking your puppy. Puppies are not born knowing that they can only relieve themselves outside. However, they do have a natural inclination to avoid going in their beds. This can, unfortunately, end with your own bed being used as a potential area to relieve himself, if you do not train him, but thankfully, there are methods that you can learn to help eliminate those negative behaviors entirely.

*W*ithin this chapter, we are going to be diving into how to housebreak your puppy. No one wants to have puppy pee and poo all over their home, so you will probably find that this is one of the first training exercises that you are going to be regularly pushing. You want to ensure that your pup is not going to have accidents all over your house, but you may not know where to begin. Thankfully, however, your resource for potty training or housebreaking your dog is here.

. . .

*W*hat to Expect

Before you begin, please note that good potty training is not instantaneous—not even close. Potty training will take time, consistency, and patience. You cannot expect to see that your dog has become fully house trained for up to a year with some of the larger breeds that tend to develop a bit slower than their smaller counterparts. Because the various breeds of dogs are so incredibly different from pup to pup, it can be really difficult to know what to expect for your specific breed. This means that you may want to stop right now and go to look up a specific guide for you. This chapter is going to be going over the basics that are going to apply for just about any dog, but if you want specifics, you will need a book dedicated to your breed.

*W*hen you begin, you are going to find that you will need to take your pup out regularly. Smaller breeds will need to go out much more frequently than larger breeds just due to being smaller and therefore having smaller bladders and higher metabolisms. Both of these translate to going regularly. Larger breeds may be able to go just a bit longer than their smaller counterparts, but not by much during those early years.

*A*s a general rule, a pup can hold its bladder for roughly one hour per year of age, plus one. We have already discussed this. However, in theory, that means that your 3-month-old dog will need you to take him out every four hours, even overnight when you may otherwise want to be sleeping. You will need to do this to meet your pup's biological need to relieve itself.

. . .

*I*n potty training, you are going to be best served learning to recognize your pet's cues and then taking him out every time you see them. Every time your pup does go outside, you will want to praise him or her heavily. You may even decide to tie some high-value treats to this activity—perhaps your pup gets a treat out of your pocket each time that he or she goes outside. In making sure that you are regularly reinforcing this behavior, you will find that your pup is much happier to go outside over time.

*H*ow to Housebreak Your Puppy

Housebreaking your puppy is quite simple—it will just take lots of time, patience, and reinforcement before your pup entirely catches onto the process. All you have to do is follow the following steps:

- Keep your pup on a schedule regularly—there should be food at very specific times each day and then remove it when that time is up. This will help regulate out his or her metabolism.

- Take your pup out first thing in the morning and every hour during the time that you are potty training. Your pup may be able to hold it for longer, but it will not help him or her really train any better if you do and you run the risk of having more and more accidents that you are trying to avoid.

- Make sure that pup goes out right before bed each and every night.

- Take the pup to the same place in your yard each tie and encourage him or her to sniff around. The smell of previous waste will linger and encourage him to go there again. This is precisely why so many pups will have the same accident in the same places indoors—they can smell their waste there.

- Always praise when your pup goes outside, followed by a high-ticket treat at first. You may try going on a walk, for example, or playing with your pup after he or she has gone.

Crate Training

Some people find that they are happiest using a crate to train their pups to go. This is because being confined in a crate activates your pup's natural instincts—they will not void where they sleep, and because you will be encouraging them to sleep in their crate, they are not likely to have accidents in there if they can avoid it at all. You will want to ensure that your pup is going out regularly, even if you keep him or her in a crate, and if you are crating, make sure that they are never in there longer than a couple of hours at a time.

. . .

*W*ith crate training, all you are going to do is place your pup in the crate for naps and when you are not actively supervising him or her. This can really help you make sure that there are no accidents around the house. When you are crate training, keep the following factors in mind:

- Make sure that your pup has enough room to stand up, turn around, and lie down comfortably. However, there should not be enough room for your pup to use a corner as a potty spot. There are crates that you can get that are entirely adjustable—you will be able to change the sizes of the siding to accommodate your pup over time so you do not have to keep buying new ones.

- If your pup is going to be crated longer than an hour or two, you must ensure that there is a freshwater dispenser present for him or her to get fresh water whenever necessary.

- If you are not home during the potty-training period, make sure that you make arrangements for someone to come in and relieve your pup if you cannot get home. For example, if you work so you cannot get home every three or four hours, try asking a neighbor if they can keep an eye on your pup. You may be surprised to find that they are totally happy to do so.

- Discontinue this method if you find that your pup regularly relieves himself in the crate. You may have a crate that is too big and your pup is not learning.

$\mathcal{U}$mbilical Training

Some people find that the best way they can train their pup to avoid accidents is a method known as umbilical training. This is exactly what it sounds like—you will want to make sure that you tether yourself to your pup so your pup cannot get up and cause trouble elsewhere. You will primarily be doing this by using a leash. At first, you may find that this is inconvenient, but over time, you may come to realize that this is actually incredibly useful to you—you will be able to use this method to ensure that your pup is not out of your sight long enough to have an accident, and you will be able to respond to your pup immediately if you do see that he is getting ready to go.

$\mathcal{W}$hen you do this, you will want to make the leash a decent length, but not long enough that your pup can slip away and out of sight. You will want to ensure that your pup is close enough that you can see him at all times. Beyond that, you simply keep your dog at your side. There is not much else to it beyond that—you just keep your pup with you as much as possible.

. . .

*I*f your pup is resistant at first, don't give in. If he has had his freedom for a while, he may assume that he can, in fact, still be given free rein to wander as he wishes. However, that is not going to work for you—you need to be able to see him to immediately get him out. If you do find that he is starting to go outside only and accidents are no longer happening, then it could be time to let him have some more autonomy. However, any time that he starts to have accidents again, he will need to be tethered to you again.

*U*sing a Bell at the Door

Some people like to train their pups to ring a doorbell when they need to go out. This allows them to sort of communicate or convey what it is that they need at any given moment. One of the best ways to do so is to get a strip of fabric or a thick rope and attach some bells to it. Then, place the bells on a hook next to the front door, low enough that your pup can reach them. Every time that you are going to go out with your pup to take him out, ring the bell. Over time, he will start to associate that sound of the bell ringing with you cuing to him that it is potty time. Over time, he will get better and better at this and he will be able to ring the bell himself when he needs to go.

*T*he trick here, however, is that you have to believe him. If he rings the bell, you go outside to let him out. You will have to do it every time so he learns the message—he learns that if he rings the bell, he gets to go to his potty spot.

TEACHING YOUR PUPPY TO FOLLOW COMMANDS

ULTIMATELY, training your puppy to follow commands is all about repetition and modeling. Over time, your pup will learn to begin to follow your commands. Training can be quite tricky to those that have never done it—pups do not inherently understand what you mean when you tell them to sit. It has to be learned over time and that can be quite tricky sometimes. We are going to go over the general process of training your pup in this chapter, going step by step to see what you need to do and what your pup will likely do at each and every step along the way.

Timeline for Training Your Pup

Training your pup can begin as soon as you have him home with you. While your pup is not going to have much in the way of an attention span yet, you are going to find that he is quite eager to please. During this juvenile stage, you are going to be teaching simple commands. You really are not working much more than teaching the rules of the house, what your pup can expect from you, and how you are going to interact with him or her. This is simple enough. This stage of training will be all about how you can interact with your pup in a gentle, positive manner and how likely you are to ensure that he or she is going to receive that message that you were trying to convey without a problem. This is more like encouraging your pup when they do happen to do what they want. You may be using treats to sort of guide the behavior, but you are not able to get them to truly understand it yet. This is like the foundation for the training that will come soon.

*I*t is not until later, when your pup is around 6 months of age that he or she will be ready for proper, formal training. This is when you can start the processes of training all of the commands that you would really like to do. This is where you will be using the proper stages that will be introduced shortly and that you will be able to expect your dog to follow on a regular basis. These different steps that you will go through will be to introduce the command, reward the command when your pup gets it right, practice and reinforce the command, and then remembering to continue to train the command and use it regularly to ensure that it is not forgotten.

*I*ntroduce the Command

The first stage here is going to be introducing the command—you are going to be deciding which command that you want your pup to know and then stating that command out loud. Especially in the early days, then, you are going to facilitate getting the pup to move into the way that you are trying to get him to. If you want to, for example, train your pup to sit, you may say, "Sit." Immediately afterward, you then use a piece of food to entice your pup to shift into a proper sitting position. You would do this simply by moving the piece of food in front of him until he looks up at it, and then continue moving it behind him. You will sort of coerce him into flopping down on his bottom in a sitting position. You will want to make sure that you only state the command once when you are trying to get the pup to obey.

Reward the Command

As soon as the pup is in the right position, it is time to reinforce it—you do this through positively rewarding the pup for doing the right thing. You give him the food, praise him, and pet him. His mind has now connected the word that you said, the food, and the positive feelings all to that behavior that you are trying to train, and that is where the power is going to be coming from.

When you reward the command, you want to make sure that your pup is rewarded with something that is going to be desirable. Over time, however, you will begin to fade out the food as a reward for following through with the behavior. You may find that what works for you is a gesture along with the treat so the gesture gets paired in there, too. No matter what the command, however, you always want to make sure that you reward it, even when it is a basic one and your pup is fully grown. You can do this with a quick verbal affirmation and a pat on the head.

Practice the Command

Next comes practice. When it is time to practice those behaviors, you are putting the mall to good use and ensuring that the pup starts to connect the word that you are using to the action that you are asking for. This is done with patience and careful encouragement. Over time, however, you will find that your pup is quite eager to follow along. Your pup will be happy to give you the result you wanted if you are willing to reward him.

*P*ractice will happen over a long period of time. Some commands may not take very much at all to reinforce but other more complex commands, such as trying to train a trick that has no real purpose other than entertainment, like playing dead in response to finger guns, will most likely take your pup much longer to figure out.

*R*einforce the Command

Reinforcement will be an important step for you. Each and every time you find that your pup is doing what you have commanded, you must make sure that you reinforce it. You can do this with anything that you want to do. All that matters is that you are making sure that your pup is catching onto your expectations and that you are making sure that your pup is interested in continuing to follow them.

*C*ontinue Use of the Command

Finally, the last step to training your pup is ensuring that he is exposed to continued use of these commands as you continue to practice them. You want to ensure that your pup knows what you want. You also want to make sure that the automatic response between your command and the action will happen regularly without much of a problem. When you do this, you will find that you will actively be encouraging your pup to remember this command.

*E*very time you repeat the command in different contexts, you will find that you are encouraging him or her to continue to remember the command. You are strengthening that connection in your mind and in doing so, you will find that you will naturally get your pup to follow along with what you want.

*W*hen you first start training, you probably chose to do so in an environment that was not particularly distracting. It could have been at your home, for example, where there is not much going on. However, at some point, you will really need to reinforce that command by practicing it in a busier setting as well. You will need your pup to know to stop and listen to you, no matter where you are or what you are doing, and because of that, you have to be able to train your pup under many different settings, reinforcing it as much as you can.

COMMANDS YOUR PUPPY NEEDS TO KNOW

AT THIS POINT, we are going to go over several of the most important commands that your pup needs to know. These commands are going to ensure that your pup is the best-behaved puppy citizen he or she can be, and that is important. Remember, a well-trained pup is a happy, healthy, safe pup, so even if you may find that the effort is a lot, it is absolutely worth it in the end. If you are not in a good place to train your pup, you may find that you are better off attempting to find someone who can. Thankfully, dog trainers are able to be found just about anywhere you go these days, so you can probably find some way to outsource the work without much trouble.

"Sit"

Perhaps the most basic command your pup can learn is the sit command. This will tell your pup to stop, plop his bottom down, and pay attention. We have already gone over the basics of this one. You will repeat the word, sit, and then take a treat right next to his nose, which you will then move up. He will follow the treat, and you will then continue to move it back. Your pup will naturally sit down when he pulls his head too far back, and at that point, you will want to shower him with all of the praise he deserves.

"Watch Me"

This command tells your pup to stop and look at you—ultimately, your pup should look to you every time that he or she is unsure what to do because you are going to be the one making that decision. This is the attention command. To do this, you are going to repeat the phrase of your choice and then offer a high ticket treat to your pup. You will start at your pup's nose with the treat and then bring it closer to yourself. Your pup should naturally follow the treat and will eventually make eye contact with you. At the eye contact, offer the treat.

"Down"

Down is a tough command to teach due to the fact that lying down is naturally a passive position to be in. They do not like being in vulnerable positions often, so you will have to work for this one. Usually, you are going to want to take a treat that smells good and show it to your pup, let your pup sniff it and then drop your hand, still holding the treat down to the floor. Slowly shift your hand away from the pup, dragging it closer to you while the up continues to sniff at the treat. As you do so, the pup will slowly follow along and you will wind up with a puppy that is eventually lying down on the floor. As soon as the pup's belly is on the floor, you say, "Down," and then offer the treat to him to reinforce it.

. . .

"Stay"

Next comes the stay command. This is incredibly important to be able to use—it tells your puppy to stop whatever he is doing and remain put. This is started by telling your pup to sit first. Your pup will naturally sit. Then, showing the treat to your pup, you will take a step backwards while repeating, "Stay." Take a few steps back. If the pup tries to get up to follow you, quickly tell him no and then move back further. Over time, you will reinforce the idea that your pup must stay put. This particular command will require a lot of reinforcement several times a day.

"Come"

The next command to work on with your pup is telling him to come along with you. This is done quite simply—put your pup in a collar and a leash and make sure that you have a treat in your hand. Say your command and pull your pup's leash a little bit. As soon as he moves forward, you then give him the treat. You will want to do this regularly as well, encouraging your pup to come on command. Eventually, you will want to try in different contexts, such as without a leash or outside.

"Drop It"

One last basic command that you may find that you need your pup to learn is to learn how to drop something on command. Whether your pup will have found an unsavory object outside, has stolen a shoe, or done anything else, you will want to make sure that your pup will let go if you tell him to. This is done by taking something that your pup likes. Perhaps you have your pup's favorite toy. Encourage your pup to take the toy in his or her mouth and then pull at it. Let your pup have it. Then, find another object that you know that your pup likes and offer that one instead. When your pup drops the first item that was in its mouth, you repeat your command and then offer the treat. This will have to be repeated regularly to get your pup to master it, but it is perhaps one of the most important. When you can tell your pup to drop something and have them do so without thinking about it, you will be able to get them to release items that they should not have. Should you find that your pup is chewing on your pants leg, you can tell your pup to drop it, and he should.

TRAINING TRICKS

WHEN YOU HAVE MASTERED some of the most basic commands that your pup can learn, you may find that you are ready to move onto something that is a bit more entertaining. You may realize that your pup loves to learn, so long as you have the right environment to facilitate it, so you decide to train some tricks.

*L*argely, these are going to be trained the same way that you would train commands. They really are no different—the only difference is that the tricks that you train are likely to be entertaining rather than functional commands that are necessary for controlling your pup. People have all sorts of reasons that they may decide to train tricks. They may find them funny or they may find them a great way to bond with their animals. No matter the reasons that you have chosen, however, you should have fun and treat them the same way that you would a command. Now, let's go over a few common tricks.

· · ·

Shake Hands

Shaking hands is quite easy to teach on command. All you have to do is make sure that you have plenty of treats on hand and the patience to walk through the process. The only command that your pup needs to know at this point is to sit down for you.

Start by instructing your pup to sit. As you do so, hold a treat in one hand, showing it to your pup. Then, close your hand so it is out of sight. Then, tell your pup, "Shake." You should then move your own fist underneath the dog's nose. He will be able to smell the treat and will most likely want it. He will most likely sniff at your paw and after a few moments, he will use his paw to touch yours. He will be trying to dig the treat out. When your pup's paw touches your hand, you then offer the treat and say, "Good."

This trick can be great for entertaining your pup, kids, and just about anyone else. It looks cool, but is not going to do much else for you beyond that. However, you may find that it is great mental stimulation for a pup that needs to be kept busy. Remember, just as with all other commands, you must make sure that your pup is getting your undivided attention and is getting reinforced regularly. You will want to repeat this process several times a day over the course of several weeks. Over time, you will find that your pet will pick up on it.

. . .

*A*fter time, you can command your pup to shake and stop offering the treat as often. You can switch the hand in which you offer the treat, for example, to start removing that association that touching the hand that was offered out is enough to get the treat. Eventually, you should be able to give the command without any real reinforcement at all.

Roll Over

Another common trick that people love is telling their pup to roll over. It is a great way to entertain children in particular, and could be a great way to help your child bond with your dog. All you will need to do this is teach your pup how to lay down. If you have that down, then the next steps will be simple.

*W*ith your pup lying down in front of you, you will want to kneel in front of him. Make sure that you have a treat in your hand as you do so. Hold the treat near his nose, but to the side somewhat. He will naturally start to sniff at the treat in your hand. Then, you are going to want to move your hand slowly, with him continuing to follow it in your hand. Move it to his shoulder and you should see him roll onto his side. Praise him at this step and offer the treat at this point in time. You are not done with the complete trick yet, but this is a great point to keep moving from.

*A*fter a few days when your pup has this particular motion down, you can then begin to continue the movement. You should no longer stop right at the shoulder but should go all the way to the backbone. He will most likely roll onto his back, at which point, you keep going until you get to the floor on the other side. He should roll all the way over at that point. Give him the treat and praise.

*W*hen he will consistently roll all the way over, you can then introduce the command that you are trying to add as well. You will have your pup perform the whole motion, then say, "Roll over," when you give him the treat, followed by praise.

*O*ver time, you will want to gradually phase out the treat and the hand motion. You may first start by eliminating the treat, and slowly then cut out the motion as well, leaving only the verbal command behind.

CORRECTING COMMON BEHAVIORAL PROBLEMS

Now, despite the cuteness of your pup, you are most likely going to find that there will be some extra hurdles for you to get over along the way. This is to be expected—your pup will want to challenge you at some point. Pups test boundaries as they age, much like children do, and because of that, you can usually wind up with some annoying behaviors that will need to be created. You will need to be able to correct these behaviors if you hope to be successful at training your pup and because of that, you may find that you need some help.

*W*ithin this chapter, we are going to go over some of the most common puppy behavioral problems that you are going to encounter, as well as how to cut down on them. Some pups will be harder than others, but if you do learn how to defeat those behaviors, you and your pup will be able to live in harmony.

. . .

Nipping

Pups don't have hands that they can use to explore the world around them, and they wind up using their mouths instead. This may be cute at first when you have a little pup that can't do much damage, but as your puppy grows in those sharp teeth, people can get hurt. Your pup is not trying to hurt you—but you do need to teach your pup that biting and nipping is not an appropriate form of play.

For young pups, you can defeat this relatively simply— start playing with your pup and let him take your hand in his mouth. As soon as he starts to bite hard enough for you to want him to stop, suddenly make a loud, high-pitched yelping sound. When you do this, you are conveying that you were hurt. Then, let your hand go limp altogether. Your pup will think that you have been hurt and because of that, he may start to lick you to help you feel a bit better. When he stops biting and starts to lick, offer praise and then continue to play.

If, after around 15 minutes, he continues to nip often, more than 3 times, you may find that you need to stop playing. Yelp and turn away altogether, ignoring him for a few seconds .When you do this, he will realize that he has been ignored and it will catch him off guard. He will feel bad and he will want to re-engage with you. After 20 seconds or show, you can start to play again.

. . .

*R*epeat this process of yelping and stopping every single time he nips too hard.

*C*hewing

Chewing is another common problem. This particular one, however, is not out of maliciousness or even being poorly behaved. Your pup is teething, and wants to chew on something. Rather than cutting out all chewing, you are going to want to make sure that your pup learns what is acceptable to chew on and what is not. This means that you will give him something that he is allowed to chew on that is entirely different from everything else around him—he should see that it is something that is distinguished from other items and entirely unique. If you use a shoe or another item that looks like another common household item, you run the risk of teaching him to look at those other similar items to chew on as well, which is not at all what you are going for right now.

*W*hile you are trying to train your pup what is acceptable, make sure that he is kept on a short leash, perhaps tethered to you, when you cannot supervise. Beyond that, make sure that he is getting plenty of exercise and going out regularly. When you do catch him chewing on something, stop him and redirect to something that he is allowed to chew on. You will want to do so by stamping your feet or clapping to startle him to make him stop before finally replacing what he was chewing on with the chew toy.

. . .

*J*umping

Puppies love us and when we come home from being away for a while, they want to say hi. They jump up to get a good smell of you and to figure out where you have been. However, as your pup gets bigger, this gets dangerous and turns into a big problem that you will need to eliminate. This means that you need to figure out how to teach your pup that all feet need to be on the ground.

*D*oing so will require you to be persistent, but is quite easy. When you walk in the door, instead of getting down for your pup to sniff at you, try entirely ignoring your pup. You will essentially tell your pup that you are not offering any positive attention until he is calm. When he is calm, you can then shower him with all of that affection that you know he wanted in the first place. You just want him to know that he cannot take it by climbing onto you.

*W*hining

Puppy whining may be cute at first, until it never stops. Whining is ultimately your pup's way of asking for help. He wants or needs something and is trying to get that in any way that he can. He may have lost his toy under the couch. He may be bored, or he may want attention. If you hear your pup whining, it would be a good idea to investigate to see if there is an easy solution. Whining makes sense if your pup needs to go out, is hungry, or needs help getting something. However, if there are no good reasons, he may be whining just to get your attention, and that is bad.

. . .

*W*hen you want to eliminate this sort of whining for your attention, then, what you are going to want to do is eliminate giving it to him altogether. He will no longer be allowed to have your attention when he whines at you. If he still does not stop whining, calmly tell him to be quiet. He may not stop right away, especially if you have not taught that as a command. Eventually, you may have to sort of snap at him—using a louder tone to make him feel like he was scolded for the whining —and then stop paying any attention to him at all.

*H*aving Indoor Accidents

Indoor accidents are something that no one wants to deal with, but are ultimately, an unavoidable part of owning a pet. When you are dealing with indoor accidents, you may feel frustrated about it. However, stop and make sure that you are firstly taking your pup out as much as possible. Make sure that you also are able to clean up the spot with a good enzyme cleaner to get as much of the smell out as possible to ensure that the scent is entirely eliminated.

*P*ups, when they can smell where they have gone before, will continue to go there because they think that is an okay place—otherwise, why would they be able to smell it? When you use a good enzyme cleaner, however, you can destroy those scents altogether. You can find these online and at your local pet store—try to find one that will work for you and you will not be disappointed. These cleaners can be used to eliminate all sorts of bacteria and stenches that you may not have even realized were there. You may even find that you will need to clean the entire floor with such a cleaner to see if there is some scent there that has been missed.

CONCLUSION

And with that, we have made it to the end of *How to Train a Puppy*. It has been a long journey, but this is really only the first step of your journey of a lifetime with your pup. You have the ability to mold your pup into developing the behavior that you would like to see from him and because of that, you should absolutely be able to enjoy your time with your pup. You can make sure that he is able to behave himself well and to ensure that you are not running into all of those bad habits that all too many dogs wind up developing somewhere along the way.

From here, all that is left is for you to put this information into use. It is no longer practice, but rather, it is solid, firm action that you need to make sure to utilize if you want to see results. Your pup, just as a child would, requires guidance. You need to be able to give your puppy the attention and guidance that he will need, and you now have the tools to do so.

Good luck on your journey into training your pup on how to behave—you should have the tools to at least get you started on the right foot! Remember, look into breed-specific resources, as this was largely a general guide for you. Finally, if you have found that this book was useful to you in any way or that the tips and tricks included within it are helping you train your new canine companion, please head over to Amazon to leave a review! It is always great to get all of that feedback.

Lightning Source UK Ltd.
Milton Keynes UK
UKHW020637121021
392080UK00013B/896